A Year of the Haiku
—*Journeying to Moonshadow*—

JAMES MAXFIELD

A Year of the Haiku
Journeying to Moonshadow
Copyright © 2021 by James Maxfield

Republished by Goto Publish on May 2021
First printing by the author, May 2014

James Maxfield, Author
Tetra Marketing Group, LLC
8445 Foraker Ct.
Mentor, Ohio 44060
440-974-8418
Email: jamesmaxfield@oh.rr.com

Library of Congress Control Number:	2021909972
ISBN-13: Paperback:	978-1-64749-466-7
ePub:	978-1-64749-467-4

All rights reserved. No part of this publication may be reproduced, distributed, or transmitted in any form or by any means, including photocopying, recording, or other electronic or mechanical methods, without the prior written permission of the publisher or author, except in the case of brief quotations embodied in critical reviews and certain other noncommercial uses permitted by copyright law.

Although every precaution has been taken to verify the accuracy of the information contained herein, the author and publisher assume no responsibility for any errors or omissions. No liability is assumed for damages that may result from the use of information contained within.

Printed in the United States of America

GoToPublish LLC
1-888-337-1724
www.gotopublish.com
info@gotopublish.com

RECOMMENDED by the USR (US Review of Books)

The US Reviews: www.theusreview.com
"A Year of the Haiku: Journeying to Moonshadow"
by James Maxfield

"After writing about ten poems... beginning on New Year's Day 2013, I decided to challenge myself to write a haiku poem every day for a year using only this finite list of words provided in the Haikubes set."

James Maxfield, a poet and teacher, received a Haikubes set for Christmas in 2012, and built a book of 365 haiku poems using the set that consists of 63 die pieces with five words on each that can form poems, meant as a brain teaser or party game. Maxfield carefully describes classical haiku—its origins in medieval Japan, its form (usually a 5-7-5 syllable three-line format) and its purpose: to create, from observing natural phenomena, a sense of universality that provokes the mind "like all good poetry." When Maxfield composed his haiku, he found that the dice choices became restrictive, so though he stuck to Haikubes words, he invented his own set of rules for combining them. He avers that to complete the task "compromise was often the order of the day."

Enjoyment of classical haiku can attain something akin to reverence. By limiting himself to the vocabulary from the Haikubes, Maxfield had to use some words that, arguably, diverge from the classical and could even offend traditionalists, such as "screwed," and one pick-your-own-profanity depicted as "#@&*#!!." This limitation not surprisingly lends the 365 offerings a wooden feel at times. Also, many of the words, and hence the poems offered, are subtly erotic, and as such may jar with classical stylists. But it's also possible that, given his restrictions, poet Maxfield had to try harder, because at their best, his creations are refreshing: "From cover of grass, / the villain, War, never sleeps— / watching by moonlight." While these poems are courageous, poets will debate if they still are haiku. Maxfield will doubtlessly excite interest with his daring experiment.

Reviewed by Barbara Bamberger Scott

This book is dedicated to my parents—

James L. Maxfield, Sr. and Dorothy Jane Maxfield

(Cover layout and design by the author)

Contents

Acknowledgements ix
Preface xi
Introduction to Haiku Poetry xvii
Source References and Notes xxv

A Year of the Haiku 1
About the Author 57

Acknowledgements

I would like to thank the following people for their help or encouragement in the completion of this book. First I would like to thank my friend John Han, a contemporary haiku poet and Professor of English at Missouri Baptist University, for his many conversations and email exchanges during the past eight years. I am also grateful for the following colleagues, friends or acquaintances who read through my introductory material and haiku poem drafts providing some constructive suggestions: My former professor and long-time friend and fellow poet, Leonard Trawick, Professor Emeritus from Cleveland State University; George Bilgere, fellow poet, who also teaches at John Carroll University near Cleveland, Ohio, and lectures on poetry at poetry readings and workshops; and my author-friend, Mark Hodermarsky, who teaches English at a private high school in Cleveland, Ohio, who has amused me greatly as my roommate for one week every summer when we meet to score AP™ English Language Essay Exams.

Preface

I am not sure how or when I first learned about haiku poems. It may be a faulty recollection that my first encounter with a haiku or haiku-like poem was fifty years ago in the mid-1960s as a junior high school student when we were given a short poem by Carl Sandburg titled "Fog" to create an artistic setting for the poem's text in art class using calligraphy.

Fog
The fog comes
on little cat feet.

It sits looking
over harbor and city
on silent haunches
and then moves on.

A few years later some short poems by e. e. cummings and perhaps the short 16-word poem by William Carlos Williams ("The Red Wheelbarrow") intrigued me enough to begin writing a few poems of my own in free verse.

Two years later, a friend and classmate introduced me to the Japanese Renga linked-verse form; and we may have even tried a few; I can't recall. But it was not until the mid-1970s as a returning college student when I was reintroduced to the two favored Japanese forms of poetry—the tanka and the haiku during one of several creative writing classes taken within a decade. So about 1977 I wrote two tanka poems (which are lost) and at least six haiku (which survive). Five of the haiku poems I entered into the college poetry contest and my entry was the second-place winner. This effort offered me the opportunity to read my poems for the poet James Dickey (who was visiting the campus and doing a poetry reading that week); he offered some favorable comments on my poetic voice and the winners of the contest were afforded the opportunity to have a three-hour lunch with the visiting poet.

These are the first haiku poems I wrote which were critiqued by James Dickey:

Five Haiku (1977)[1]

Petite white roses,
and remember yesterday—
the altar, the bride.

Dandelion wine,
two cups—but you passed me by
sweet honeysuckle.

The snow blows all ways,
red leaves turning in the cold,
membering the graves.

Music in the sun—
the murmuring hummingbird . . .
still the crow caws, caws.

The smell of lilies—
flowered memories lying
dead on the coffin.

During the next thirty-odd years I think I may have only written another handful of haiku poems. So to write a book of 365 haiku poems seems an unlikely undertaking and requires this brief explanation. For the Christmas of 2012 I received a gift of the *Haikubes*[2] set of 63 die pieces containing five words on each die piece. I have seen similar game-like ideas for creating short poems as a creative writing teaching method for children or adults. But this set was specifically for writing haiku poems. The basic idea is to scatter the cubes or roll them like dice then select 8 or 12 of the cubes and create or assemble a poem from the words showing on the top face of each cube chosen at random.

After writing about ten poems (one each day) beginning on New Year's Day 2013, I decided to challenge myself to write a haiku poem every day for a year using only this finite list of words provided in the *Haikubes* set. This was actually quite a challenge. Not only are there a limited set of words (about 315 words—five words on each of 63 cubes), but some words were repeated, and some words were not very good words for poetry—that is—some words were difficult words to use for poetry. There were also about three dozen words that were prepositions, articles, or conjunctions—fill words. Consequently, there were perhaps only 275 core words to select from to create 365 haiku poems, and there seemed to be only a handful of verbs—another challenge. Just doing some simple arithmetic will show that in order to create 365 poems, each key word would have to be used an average of 30 times during the sequence. So the challenge here would be to try to use words in different ways or senses and in different settings, themes, or combinations. (Though I must admit that I did not dwell too much on this; but I tried to do it unconsciously.)

The first thirty poems seemed to go rather well before I began to find that the words showing face up on 10 or 12 dice were not providing enough inspiration, so I began to "cherry pick" and look for the word I wanted from the rest of the cubes. This hunt and peck approach was used for the next 75 poems or so; then I had to get more creative and began to make up my own rules as I went. The first rule was that I allowed myself to use any form of the word showing on a cube. So for example, for the word "glorious" I was also allowed to use: glory, glories gloried, or gloriousness. In other words, I could make a noun into an adjective or a verb or make a word plural or singular as needed or change the tense of a verb as desired.

This approach seemed to work fine until I reached about 220 poems; then I needed a new approach. I had realized that at any one time I really only had the use of about 50 words if I limited my word choices to only one side of a cube at a time. In other words, in this manner, words on the same cube would never be used in the same poem. I thought this unfair and too limiting. So to "expand" the available words I created a kind of chessboard chart and randomly put all of the words of each cube into squares on my chessboard. Most squares had words from only one cube. I further divided and placed all of the prepositions, adjectives, and conjunctions in separate squares to find them more easily when needed. The one rule I did not violate was to add words by using a word that was not in the set of given words. Although, during my final proofreading of the poems, I found several poems that violated my own rule—but I decided to let them go.

Using my "chessboard" grid of word choices for the remainder of the poems, I moved around the board horizontally, vertically, diagonally, in L-shaped patterns, and random patterns in groups of three squares at a time until I had finished all 365 poems. The poems were written for the most part in the order presented in this book, except for a few odd poems that I moved for the arbitrary reason that I accidently used the same word twice in one week, which I considered an "unwritten rule" and tried to avoid. Here is my "chessboard" grid of words from the *Haikubes* set:

Haikubes Word List

Clever, mature, precious, dynamic, glorious	Slimy, able, dead, wise, friendly	Flesh, body, light, candy, time	Flying, swimming, dreaming, eats, opens	Went, blows, spat, slips, whispers
My, me, us, he, she, his, her, our, Your, I, We, you, it's, what, who, it's, what, who, they, it,	Oozing, feeling, touches, sleeping, mouthing Putrid, sleep, lurid, ravenous, happy, alternate	Have, tried, shot, screwed, greased Love, yelled, hoped, embraced, Into, shape, shines	Wicked, silly, sneaky, gorgeous, pregnant, shiver, fall, killed, licks, ran, so, after, before, so not	Next, last, behind, inside, with, to, in, Out, between, up, under, on, over, along, around, of, down, across, for
Which, its, a, an, as, this, that, or, those, the, these	Boy, man, girl, lips, woman, lots,	One, many, any, but, through, never, if, no, all	Logical, balance, fertile, simple, swell	Too, also, not, every, left, right, wrong, wild, wet

A Year of the Haiku

Promises, sees, watching, rides, looks	Eyes, cheeks, ass, hand, limbs, tiger, places, nerve	Crack, bust, lame, trunk, peace, hump, torture	War, sucker, noodle, partner, fortune	Stick, god, pool, muck, ouch
Calls, biting, sang, dancing, dripping	Revolting, curvy, sour, sweet, salty,	Point, clamor, hero, grace, stage,	Parallel, melodic, radical, hell-bent, shady, doctor	Villain, thugs, honestly,
Heavy, smooth, hot, hard, fast, livid, lofty, anal	Bottle, charm, shelter, heart, thunder, doctor	There, bank, here, home, room, science	Fathom, overlook, realize, wind, following	Travel, glancing, pluck, return, ritual
Grand, clear, cover, violet, gentle,	Waste, grass, fire, water, life,	Spiral, flock, blocks, ground, journey,	Marvel, surface, prick, window, finger,	Etc, hmmmm, -esque, #@&*#!!
Giant, moonlight, fantasy, trouble Dilemma, riches	Slowly, desperate, finally, quickly, timidly, turn, must	Consume, switch,	Obey, leaves, stay, please, tangle,	Mommy, daddy, baby, sister, brother,
Gleeful, empty, full, mouthful, ugly	World, romantic, life, childhood,	Family, work, future	Reflection, vision, dream, desire,	Tirade, regret

    Besides using only words or forms of words from the list above to compose these haiku poems, I consciously adhered to the basic 5-7-5 syllables per each three-line poem. However, as you will note after reading the following Introduction to Haiku Poetry, a strict adherence to counting syllables is not always followed. So during the editing process, I deleted some articles or words that seemed to be fill-words, words that did not contribute to the poem or that detracted from its sense of "compactness" or natural rhythm. I also noticed during the editing process that upon retrospection and reconsideration, the poems written by the process of "dice-rolling" (the first 225 or so poems) required more revision and editing than the later poems written using my "chessboard" grid. It seems that "chance" is a less effective strategy than a more formal writing system.

A Note on Punctuation

It seems common that many contemporary haiku poets use a minimum of punctuation. Since haiku poems were written as original Japanese or Chinese characters that required no punctuation, Western punctuation was introduced during the translation process of classical haiku poetry. There are good arguments for both using and not using or in minimizing punctuation. In this collection of haiku I have tried to consistently use punctuation (including dashes, hyphens, and ellipses) where needed: to separate ideas or thoughts or images; to slow down the reader or speaker; to emphasize a word or phrase or as a parenthetical (a dash or dashes); to signify the continuation of something after a pause of missing time (ellipsis); or to merge the meaning of two words into one (hyphen). Thus, the style and uses of punctuation in my haiku writing are similarly consistent with how I write other forms of poetry.

Final Comment

Naturally, some of the poems here may "fail" because the word or words I would have liked to use in some cases were either not available from the list of given words or I had used that word already within the current week. Compromise was often the order of the day. I would write around the word I really wanted to use or I would change the poem entirely—which sometimes would lead to an inspired and expected discovery, but sometimes to a dead end. Although I am not entirely content with every poem that resulted from this exercise of word constraint, I hope there may be enough good poems here to please the reader. In order to appreciate haiku poetry more fully, I have taken some pains below to include a substantial summary of the history and conventions of haiku poetry writing.

James Maxfield, March 2014

Introduction to Haiku Poetry

The haiku, this favored Japanese poetic form, was introduced to the Western world after 1900, but it was not until after the Second World War that the haiku form became influential as a kind of fixed form for American poets. During the 1950s and 1960s, the Beat and the Hippie Generations in America became fascinated with haiku poetry, principally as the result of a proliferation of new anthologies and translations of Japanese poetry along with an increased awareness and interest in Eastern religions and philosophy, especially Zen Buddhism. These two generations of students and writers were attracted to haiku poems for their apparent "brevity and seeming simplicity."[3] They usually contain only one or two sentences (sometimes fragments); however, they generally only employ one poetic image—usually expressed with vivid, descriptive language and "clarity of vision."[4] As with all good poetry, haiku should express an exalted and intensified experience that exhibits a greatly controlled "subtlety of its effects."[5]

The haiku poem underwent continuous development and refinement throughout the centuries of Medieval Japan. Haiku poems were originally used as the introductory poem setting to another poem (the *Tanka*) and written in sequences of varying lengths called *Renga* with prescribed "rules" and conventions for linking tanka and haiku poems together in long sequences composed by two alternating poets. Toward the end of the Heian Period in Medieval Japan (794-1185), Japanese poets began to separate the haiku portion of the 5-line tanka poems and to write them specifically as stand-alone poems apart from the Renga linked-verse sequences.[6]

By the 16th century in Japan both haiku and tanka poems were well-established as stand-alone poems, and by the 19th century this was more or less commonplace as the Renga sequences declined in popularity. The familiar haiku form of the 3-line poem structure adhering to a sequential counting of 5-7-5 syllables per line remains dominant even today—despite the free use of variations and departures of this norm by many contemporary haiku poets. The more serious classical Japanese traditional haiku poetry also gave way by the 19th century to employ humor and irony to describe everyday situations or observations. But haiku poems that are overtly funny may more properly be called *Senryu*, and many contemporary haiku poets tend to write mostly in this manner.

Poetic Structure and Haiku Conventions

R. L. Blyth, one of the most well-known of all American haiku scholars, indicates the term "haiku" (formerly hokku and haikai) comes into use during the Meiji Period of Japan (1868-1912) as a poem structure of 5-7-5 syllable lines and totaling 17 syllables in the poem.[7] The use of 17 syllables may have significance for being the typical number of syllables the poet can speak (or sing) in one breath; and the use of the 3-lines may symbolize a "feeling of ascent, attainment, and resolution of [the poetic] experience."[8] Since the 8th or 9th centuries in Japan, the haiku poem was used to begin the tanka poem. The 5-line tanka poem structure begins with a haiku poem of three lines (5-7-5 syllables per line) and finishes with 2 lines of 7 syllables each to conclude the poem. These final two lines generally function as a self-reflection upon or by the poet himself as he writes about his subject (usually nature). Eliminating these two lines of the tanka tended to remove the poet from the poem, thus breaking "the self-reflective mirror, leaving in the hands of the poet only the mirror that reflects nature."[9]

Regarding poetic rhyme in Japanese poetry, when poems are "said" or "sung" there are no accented syllables per se as in Western poetry,[10] where we differentiate accentual verse by counting the spoken stresses or unstressed syllables that delineate specific meters, such as iambic pentameter, which is often asserted to be the most natural meter for English poetry. Scanning any number of haiku poems in English one may find that the accents will often be two accented syllables in the first and third shorter lines and three accents in the middle line. But there is no rule regarding this. On the subject of syllable-counting, the well-regarded Beat Poet, Kenneth Rexroth, in his haiku translations [and in his own poems] says he has "always striven for *maximum compression* (emphasis mine)—eliminating unnecessary words or syllables, freely deviating from the 5-7-5 syllabic format as needed.[11]

One result of the general inattention to accented words or syllables is the relative aversion in haiku writing to some forms of repetition, such as alliteration and end-rhyme words, as well as many of the typical poetic conventions found in Western poetry and other repetitive devices like anaphora (the repetition of first words or sounds in successive lines). The rhyming of words in particular also has no place in traditional classic haiku poetry; although in original Japanese language poetry and haiku, there are often patterns of repeating vowel sounds (assonance), especially vowels that end each line or the repetition of words within a line (also a common rhetorical device).[12] But these effects are seldom seen in translations or new haiku written in English or other languages.

In addition to the simple 5-7-5 syllabic form, another classical Japanese haiku convention was the almost obligatory or at least customary reference (either directly or indirectly) to one of the four seasons of nature. This feature is arguably one that is often ignored in modern haiku poems. In early Medieval Japan, the tanka form of 5-7-5-7-7 syllable lines became "codified" as the preferred poetic form for Japanese poetry written at court by nobleman and samurai warriors—who wrote poems in praise of their observations of nature and the landscape (mountains, rivers, trees), but poems gradually included a "subtext of human emotion" and a sense of season. As haiku poems were increasingly written by Zen monks, the emotional element became less important and subordinate to simple observations of nature.[13]

Johanna Brownell remarks in the introduction to her concise edition of famous classical Japanese haiku poems that haiku poetry, though somewhat austere in composition, can evoke emotion from simple everyday observations using concrete descriptions expressing the simple "purity and beauty of nature." The subject matter of haiku poems frequently focus on the seasons, the moon, animals, flowers, birds, weather—essentially all of nature, including human nature and human interactions—although this is arguably more prominent in modern and contemporary haiku.[14] Kenneth Rexroth summarizes that typical themes or subjects for classical haiku can be found in "autumn leaves, falling snow, plum or cherry blossoms, the moon in its phases and seasons, the rustle of leaves," insect and animal sounds, ceremonial occasions, poems for lovers, and many others.[15]

According to Stephen Addis, the haiku poem focuses "upon a small aspect of nature rather than the larger landscape."[16] Addis further asserts the haiku poet treats conventional themes and subjects both *visually* and *verbally* within the poetic setting and by his word choices.[17] While it is uncommon to use war, sex, natural disasters (or anything that would harm nature, animals, or humans) as haiku subjects for poems,[18] some poets and critics have considered this a shortcoming of the haiku form. But in contemporary or modern haiku, few if any subjects would be considered off-limits today. Blyth groups haiku subjects into five general categories of poems that: record sensations, portray scenes from life, portray ourselves, express human warmth, and romantic verses.[19]

The Making of Haiku Poems

The cornerstone of poetry is often asserted to be the use of comparisons of unlike things. But haiku poetry places less reliance on the use of metaphoric comparisons and similes. However, the use of "fixed epithets" that are similar to the Homeric similes and metaphors of classic Western verse traditions can also be found in Japanese poetry,[20] such as this simple compounded comparison: *a many-starred night*. One characteristic of most poetry that is also common in haiku is the use of a "pivot" word that can be interpreted or read in two different senses or meanings (as in double meanings). Such uses can be one of several variety of typical rhetorical devices, such as irony for a surprise twist or ending, and frequently it may be used as a simple pun for a humorous effect.[21]

Blyth notes that (in 1958) a Japanese publication on haiku poetry asserted that "most contemporary haiku poets believe that haiku is symbolistic, that is, it seeks to represent ideas and emotions by indirect suggestion, and to attach a symbolic meaning to particular objects."[22]

But Blyth elsewhere seems to disagree and strongly argues that the core essence of the haiku poem not have any symbolic meanings inferred from the poem apart from the natural scene being described.[23] Western poets steeped in their own English, American, or European poetic and literary traditions have difficulty with this—and find it difficult to write poetry devoid of the conscious use of literary devices or techniques or in using metaphoric meanings and symbolism—which are as natural for them as breathing.

Classic or traditional haiku poems generally conform to these three basic conventions: the poem describes a single event or scene; the time is usually in the present (although in the Zen sense, there is no time—all time is the same—past, present, and future); and there is a seasonal reference.[24] The expression of time in haiku poetry may be the result of the Zen concept of "impermanence"—that nature, seasons, life, landscapes—all things—are subject to change. Reflecting on this notion of impermanence naturally leads to poetic reflection and "pensive verses."[25] The famous haiku poet of the 17th century (Basho) focused his poetic "gaze on nature and the living creatures around him [. . .] and captured the meeting between the universal pulse of nature and the intensely human aesthetic perception of a particular time and space." He says: "Humans don't control nature, they are in harmony with nature."[26]

Haiku, like all good poetry, should attempt to garner or glean "the essence of a moment's experience [. . .] say[ing] more than the sum of its words, leading the reader into the practice of understanding the great [truth or insight that is] unsaid that is contained, framed in the poem's rhythms, words, and silences. In these ways [haiku] opens the mind"[27] so that we try to appreciate that "the haiku poet observes what others scarcely see."[28] The haiku poet strives to become unconscious of himself and "to see the object of his poem with absolute clarity [and] to say something indirectly[29] by implication or extension—or in the words of Emily Dickinson—to "say it slant." According to Professor Hoffman, "that which remains unsaid [in the haiku poem] tells more than the words and yet is unclear without [the words].[30] It is the conciseness and compactness of the haiku poem that allows the image of the poem to stand out in stark contrast against the white of the page, permitting the reader to fill in the space with meaning or to complete the image or the scene with his own imagination, thus allowing for infinite meaning.

The Way of the Haiku

The ancient Japanese poet approached the writing of haiku in much the same manner as a Samurai warrior would approach the care and use of his sword, his bow and arrows, his armor, or his philosophy and religion—with careful consideration and mindful reflection—an attentiveness to form and execution of practice; a form of meditation; and as a way of living in the present in harmony with all living things (great and small) within the universe.

During the 18th and 19th centuries in Japan, haiku poetry developed its Zen-like flavor or predisposition, which to a large degree became commonplace in classical haiku writing of this period; but many contemporary haiku writers are not so attuned. Before the 1950s in America, "Zen" was a relatively unknown term when the Beat Generation writers embraced it along with the ethos of the philosophy of Zen-Buddhism and popularized it in their fiction, poetry, and essays.[31] What is Zen Poetry? What is a Zen haiku poem? Blyth indicates the presence of an "unspoken creed of the haiku poets [that] love of nature is religion, and religion is poetry; these three things are one thing."[32] More recently, Sam Hamill in his book *The Poetry of Zen* sums it up as "nothing other than an expression of the enlightened mind, a handful of simple words that disappear beneath the moment of insight to which it bears witness."[33]

Blyth alludes to the idea that in haiku poetry writing, two ideas or concepts seem to merge together at three levels: 1. The poet and the poem become "one"; 2. The poem itself seems to embody or take on the sensations elicited by the words and images in the poem; and 3. The spiritual essence of the poem can be apprehended by reading or looking at the poem's text—each syllable, word, phrase, or line represents *at once* the experience of the poem. This is perhaps due in part that the original composition of haiku were in Japanese or Chinese pictorial characters, which are "read" visually as drawings, as well as how these figures translate into phrases.[34]

Blyth defines the approach to haiku in a manner very Japanese-like by referring to "The Way of Haiku, which is the purely poetical (non-emotional, non-intellectual, non-moral, non-aesthetic) life in relation to nature"[35]—it is "a perpetual sinking of oneself into things"—your observations and experiences of the everyday life.[36]

According to Blyth, haiku poetry "must express a new or newly perceived sensation, or sudden awareness of the meaning of some common human experience of nature or man. Furthermore, the haiku poem must "not be explanatory or contain a cause and effect" [relationship].[37] Blyth refers to a letter by the haiku scholar, J. W. Hackett, who argues that haiku writing is essentially an "existential experience rather than a literary exercise in poetic form—that haiku writing is an "intuitive experience." Hackett supports this idea with a quote from the famous Japanese haiku poet Basho: "Haiku is simply what is happening in this place at this moment."[38]

The Zen-like quality of haiku poetry that I most appreciate and try to invoke or emulate myself is the sense that whether listening to or writing, reading, or saying the poem, it is a form of meditation that *absorbs* both the poet and the audience and may lead one to a state of "self-realization and wisdom.[39] One Zen-like theme that may be observed in haiku is the assertion that the "only permanence is impermanence; and where change [. . .] remains the essence of being";[40] and this "Zen essence is expressed elegantly and succinctly."[41] Blyth expresses it this way: The independently-written haiku poem of itself has developed a poetic voice that beams with an "eye-opening, startling realization that approaches the Zen notion of a sudden enlightened experience.[42] The Zen approach to haiku writing "embodies the spirit of Zen [by] celebrating the world [as it is] seen instead of the poet as its lone [or lonely] observer.[43]

"Haiku shows us what we knew all the time,
but did not know we knew [it]."[44]

Source References and Notes

1. These poems were lost in a fire in 1999 but were reconstructed from memory with a slight revision to one or two poems.
2. Forrest-Pruzan Creative, *Haikubes*, (San Francisco: Chronicle Books).
3. Stephen Addis, and Fumiko and Akira Yamamoto, *Haiku Landscapes: In Sun, Wind, Rain, and Snow*, (Trumbull, CT: Weatherhill, 2002) 7.
4. Yoel Hoffman, ed., *Japanese Death Poems*, (Boston: Tuttle Publishing, 1986) 22.
5. Kenneth Rexroth, *One Hundred Poems from the Japanese*, 26th printing (New York: New Directions Publishing, 1955,) ix.
6. Hoffman 15-16.
7. R. H. Blyth, A *History of Haiku: Volume Two,* (Tokyo: Hokuseido P, 1963) xii.
8. Blyth, *History, Vol. Two*, 351.
9. Hoffman 20.
10. Rexroth xiii.
11. Rexroth x.
12. Rexroth xv-xvi.
13. Addis *Haiku Landscapes*,7-8.
14. Johanna Brownell, ed., *Haiku: Seasons of Japanese Poetry*, (Edison, N. J.: Book Sales, Inc., 2004) Introduction.
15. Rexroth xii.
16. Addis, *Landscapes*, 7.
17. Addis Landscapes, 10.
18. R. H. Blyth, *A History of Haiku: Volume One,* (Tokyo: Hokuseido P, 1963) 4.
19. R. H. Blyth, *The Genius of Haiku: Readings from R. H. Blyth on Poetry, Life, and Zen*. James Kirkup, ed. (Tokyo: Hokuseido P, 1995) 94.
20. Rexroth xv.
21. Rexroth xvi-xvii.
22. Blyth, *History, Vol. One*, 13.
23. Blyth, *Genius*, 71.

24. Hoffman 26.
25. Stephen Addis, and Fumiko and Akira Yamamoto, *A Haiku Menagerie: Living Creatures in Poems and Prints,* (New York: Weatherhill, 1992) 8.
26. Addis, *Menagerie*, 9.
27. Sam Hamill, and J. P. Seaton, eds. *The Poetry of Zen.* (Boston: Shambhala, 2004) 5.
28. Hoffman 26.
29. Hoffman 24.
30. Hoffman 24.
31. Hamill 1.
32. Blyth, *Genius*, 85.
33. Hamill, front leaf.
34. Blyth, *History, Vol. One*, 7
35. Blyth, *Genius*, 15.
36. Blyth, *Genius*, 30.
37. Blyth, *History, Vol. One*, 11.
38. Blyth, *History, Vol. Two*, 351.
39. Hamill 1.
40. Hamill 3.
41. Hamill, 5.
42. Blyth, *History, Vol. One*, 2
43. Blyth, *History, Vol. One*, 6.
44. Blyth, *Genius*, 63.

A Year of the Haiku
— Journeying to Moonshadow —

1.
Wild sleep, this partner—
my desperate promises . . . one
dynamic shiver.

2.
Across wise water,
you under this moonlight—
turning to look.

3.
What villainous lips—
the precious wind licks slowly
our wet promises.

4.
The clever hero
follows timidly, looking
gently in clover.

5.
Sheltered down shady
cracks of many stages tried—
watching gleefully.

6.
Fortune lights it clear—
Grace never sang so sweetly . . .
following a fall.

7.
In granite and marble
we shelter the dead from war—
gently fall the leaves . . .

8.
Pregnant fantasy—
into violet riches . . .
never before you.

9.
Dancing through whispers,
dreaming inside of moonlight,
trying something new.

10.
Behind, thunder slips
along the ground; ravenous,
hell-bent calls sound clear.

11.
This radical crack
marks the surface, traveling . . .
parallel fortunes.

12.
The last smooth shape went
dripping through lofty windows
oozing sweet promises.

13.
Your cheeks wet with charm,
a mouthful of fertile leaves
covered in clover . . .

14.
Glorious thunder—
drowning under simple sleep,
flies the hell-bound wind.

A Year of the Haiku

15.
An empty bottle—
Time swells, tangles your fortune
in pools of water.

16.
Return fantasy,
spiraling into balance—
Time's hand slips, watching.

17.
With every wrong
it's wicked to realize
how her heart consumes.

18.
Desperate voices
mouthing a melodic song—
simple rituals.

19.
Pools of water
watch across lofty overlooks
dreaming of journey.

20.
Moonlit surface sleeps
following behind thunder—
this violet night.

21.
A fantasy drips
water, honestly embraced—
empty mouthfuls.

22.
It is oozing pluck,
that gentle, wise wind . . . heavy
with your greased whispers.

23.
Parallel partners,
fertile lips with wild whispers
thunder down on flesh.

24.
Around each new turn
those sweet, melodic voices
ride along the wind.

25.
Ravenous for sleep,
traveling along home—
watching the tiger.

26.
Lofty wings flying,
clamoring at my window—
trouble slips hard by . . .

27.
Alternate fortunes:
living on empty, dead last . . .
desperate leaves.

28.
Prickfuls of wild looks
slip softly behind cover—
lips mouthing moonlight.

29.
Whispers flying clear,
fast behind tangled eyes . . . hmmmm—
watching thunder sleep.

30.
Every journey
between places—lame promises—
turns moonlight and leaves.

31.
Wild through dripping sleep,
sour candy for a baby—
trouble licks its grace.

32.
Touching heavy ground,
sheltered peace consumes, watching
the cover surround.

33.
Dynamic balance—
your science clear, dripping wet
with salty mouthfuls.

34.
Doctor your fertile
heart between banks of moonlight,
the last leaves blown dead.

35.
Desperate travels
spiral here to realize—
Time switches places.

36.
It slowly opens,
wild, tiger-love returns—
violet woman.

37.
Shivering between
clear, lame, lofty promises
before switching lots.

38.
Smooth, friendly touches
timidly alternate—now
trying slow torture.

39.
What coverable
charms you have; hard-embraced grass
under the window.

40.
Your violet peace
looks around precious places—
under tangled love.

41.
Swimming in moonlight
slowly through a cracked window—
the simple dripping . . .

42.
Flying parallel,
shivering through lofty winds
watching the tiger.

43.
Shady dilemma—
the looks have you embraced . . .
revolting finger.

44.
Behind curvy shapes,
following a fantasy—
marveled dancing hearts.

45.
What we realize
along violet whispers—
hmmmm . . . the waste of time . . .

46.
That desperate wind—
wicked, ravenous lips pricked
around, hard-embraced.

47.
Following tangles
of flesh—fire behind wild eyes,
clamors of thunder.

48.
Your charm shines empty—
a logical ritual . . .
so not hoped for that.

49.
From cover of grass,
the villain, War, never sleeps—
watching by moonlight.

50.
Precious desires—
water-dreaming, fathoms down
gracing dead whispers.

51.
Those sweet promises
torture my heart—glancing blows
dancing along home.

52.
Across empty ground,
to friendly places return—
we all dream of home.

53.
Our world, revolting
life, desperate for empty
sleep—with opened the eyes.

54.
Flying, villain wind—
Must wise lips crack so with love? . . .
torture of whispers . . .

55.
Following after—
my oozing timidity:
your wet, biting lips.

56.
He marvels that bust,
its spiral love shapes woman—
between promises.

57.
Pooling precious light
licks with melodic touches,
must shape the wild heart.

58.
Childhood promises—
you sleeping thugs; salty lips
stuck hard over time.

59.
Shining reflections
oozing between fantasies—
eyes of fire consume.

60.
A childhood regret
yells, runs . . . so not mature—I
return there flying.

61.
The bottle drips clear,
quickly leaves the last mouthful,
wets that hell-bent wind.

62.
On dancing water
fertile pools of glancing light—
empty hearts singing.

63.
That lofty feeling—
watching from pregnant places,
unreturnable.

James Maxfield

64.
A consumed bottle,
ravenous flocks flying through—
shady, slimy grass.

65.
A silly regret—
my heavy travel trunk falls—
all your simple charms.

66.
My wicked fortune
curving between simple shapes—
shady, clever flesh.

67.
A precious childhood
gently embraces, opens,
slipping between cracks.

68.
Your grand rituals,
my empty, parallel limbs . . .
fertile fantasies.

69.
Feeling across fire,
fast she opens there, between
my dancing fingers.

70.
Tried sleeping around
every empty shelter—
finally smooth ground.

71.
Happy trouble—wild,
her gorgeous body swimming—
sweet, dripping journey.

72.
Violet lips call,
your slim, spiraled limbs shining—
God, I tried to sleep.

73.
Flying after life
—oozing pools, banks of riches—
water licks between.

74.
A revolting crack—
a boy hero rides above
the grand overlook.

75.
As wind in the grass
watches parallel bodies—
slowly trunks tangle.

76.
Slow finger-touches,
love's ritual winds around,
timidly opens . . .

77.
Wild clamoring,
dancing shapes, clever children—
mommy watching there.

78.
Slowly our childhood
slips time; sticks and promises
pluck across the stage.

79.
Across our tired world,
my lofty dreams blowing sweet
spirals . . . dripping lips.

80.
Those sweet baby licks,
happy all sleeping inside
between glancing looks.

81.
Through pregnant dreaming,
tangled tigers, shady grass—
our violet riches.

82.
A prickly wind
before promises—feeling
along her cheeks . . .

83.
She rides home a dream
up gentle spiral shelters—
hmmmm . . . sleeping slowly.

84.
Regrets about you—
love also never leaves room . . .
troubles my left turn.

85.
We never charm those
radical brothers—biting,
mouthing our sweet shot.

86.
Feelings alternate,
last stages of reflection—
ground under sweet grass.

87.
What clear, full moonlight
opens to a friendly wind,
slipping slowly through . . .

88.
Clever shapes tangle,
ride heavy upon the heart—
time turns to dripping . . .

89.
That villain, Regret,
pricking with ravenous hand—
hmmmm, here I shiver.

90.
To travel a world
inside my room, I embrace
wild, lofty places.

91.
The doctor calling—
a melodic pools of grace . . .
gorgeous girl baby.

92.
Under a fertile
fortune, your shiver covers
before spiral winds.

93.
The clamor of gods,
brother villains, so heavy
with glorious man.

94.
Slowly oozing life,
a clear, dynamic consumes
timid winds, whispers . . .

95.
Our wild, livid world
tries simple, shady cover—
putrid flesh, limbs . . .

96.
Pluck-able fortunes
slip along every
ugly crack of war.

97.
Gorgeous eyes watching
whispers of love; simple grace—
too hot, her bottle.

98.
Troubled dreaming—
clamor at the window turns
tangled promises.

99.
Down empty blocks
a mature muck consumes us—
shady, putrid waste.

100.
A dream . . . light sleeping
between giant spiral rides . . .
swells my salty eyes.

101.
Her heart sees within:
dilemmas for the dead—
fired shapes flying lame.

102.
A prick on the cheek—
ouch! Then they turn with sweet slips
on wet lips, glancing.

103.
That point of balance—
radical, sleeping bodies,
looks—empty, heavy . . .

104.
Revolting thunder
returns—shoots along a nerve—
your sucker-biting.

105.
This wicked wind yells,
dances over what dead waste;
warring desires.

106.
A desire for home,
you journey after water—
those oozing riches.

107.
Your eyes, fertile charms,
have honestly overlooked
the next dilemma.

108.
Gorgeous reflection—
curvy, desperate body:
the sleeping tiger . . .

109.
A wicked vision . . .
timidly revolting, calls,
touches places clear . . .

110.
Through putrid, wet waste
—wicked, anal parallels—
shines stages of war.

111.
God—moonlight places . . .
we never realize there,
the shelter of peace.

112.
Desperate return—
trouble swimming all along
that empty heart-bank.

113.
A boy, swimming through
violet waste—wet, soured ground—
the science of muck.

114.
Turn under water—
she hoped your point logical.
Try any window . . .

115.
Glorious body—
wild, her ravenous, smooth charms . . .
a gorgeous tiger.

116.
Her sucker-biting
baby, feeling for riches . . .
hmmmm . . . she eats at last.

117.
Its logical point—
ugly dreaming about waste,
leaving fantasy.

118.
Quickly one licks clear
across every surface—
slimy, salty pools . . .

119.
We whisper on home
following promises; love
those melodic winds.

120.
Putrid, dead waste through
dynamic hard-ass blocks, swells
my anal dreaming.

121.
Wild visions about
watching tangled noodles hump—
with lame, dripping flesh.

122.
Pregnant calls, empty . . .
with one livid, violet
shot; sleep consumes me.

123.
Emptied slowly—she
shot there every wicked
woman, sister-killed.

124.
A fingered bottle
following moonlight marvels—
clear, right-able pluck.

125.
Curvy eye candy—
licking along the surface,
a ravenous man.

126.
Watching over flocks,
a gentle, precious sister
shines before her time.

127.
Fertile, life partners—
a marvelous she-tiger . . .
her too hard body.

128.
Oozing pluck, slowly
that greased stick returns with thugs—
clearly . . . dripping . . .

129.
Dynamic, full shapes
turn between parallel hearts—
friendly, wet looks.

130.
With ravenous licks
flocking across alternate points;
her lips embrace peace.

131.
I slip through tangled
rooms following after you—
sneaky, curvy limbs.

132.
Love: melodic, sweet
dancing under full cover—
sleeping gods shiver.

133.
Clever dilemma:
so not light for promises . . .
your wind on my cheeks.

134.
It returns, it stays
feeling between violets
the moonlight clamor.

135.
She tried to fathom,
with all limbs flying over
her silly mommy.

136.
A pooled reflection
looks before a shady bank,
licking ground bottles.

137.
A mouthful of dream,
curvy lips dripping on down
her friendly body.

138.
Our dynamic world,
a lurid, lofty villain,
that sleeping giant.

139.
She spirals slowly,
ritualesque . . . blows gently—
this hard dilemma.

140.
What clamor of grass . . .
Must leaves prick this lasting peace?
Simple tortured love.

141.
Biting lips pricked full,
salty water-swells never
turn along to home.

142.
Moonlight reflections
sleep—Have any embraced it,
that gentle clamor?

143.
Those next killed by her
lips, between desperate turns—
dead, tangled eyes see.

144.
Troubled peace, sweet war—
a life through whispering rooms—
thugs block my return.

145.
Its last licks, dripping,
slip hard upon slimy cheeks—
water-watching time . . .

146.
Desire watches there—
your sheltered feelings whisper,
fingering with pluck.

147.
Ritual fasting
—alternate desires for flesh—
Fathoms any fire.

148.
A wind, hmmmm-ing along,
its clever grace pricks my cheeks—
my future, troubled.

149.
Shady, tangled lips
I tried—next, mouthfuls of grass—
her thunder places.

150.
A pregnant vision
turns slowly, swimming around
a glorious god.

151.
Her fortune looks hot.
Who ran after that doctor?
This up-lit journey . . .

152.
Finally peace shines
here—sweet biting, my touches . . .
one simple whisper.

153.
For a dancing girl
sucker violets open—
glancing, gleeful eyes.

154.
The last able man
must muck along over her
sweet thunder of war.

A Year of the Haiku

155.
Wild by ground-fire killed,
these ravenous rituals,
our violet cheeks.

156.
Fire-shapes flock over
empty pools—desperate for
shady she-doctor.

157.
Grand fantasies—
sweet, ravenous licks consume
with grace . . .one fast girl.

158.
. . . realizing that
watching through wicked windows
never touches you . . .

159.
Is anybody home?
Every clever heart slips
embracing her.

160.
Fertile rituals—
opening wet, tangled wars . . .
our lame world dripping . . .

161.
Across livid eyes,
a regret about my brother—
torture, so not wise.

162.
Between gleeful limbs,
her fortune slipping inside
of wet swimming trunks . . .

163.
Swollen rituals—
oozing moonlit ground embraces
shady reflections.

164.
Romantic sleep, sweet
—after many a stayed light—
from clamoring lips.

165.
Desperate places—
this mature wind, hot thunder . . .
a sneaky finger.

166.
Down a gentle bank
through pools of dead promises—
under waterfalls.

167.
Happy, dancing worlds—
but before grace is emptied
last—parallel lots.

168.
A reflection on
love—desperate, dynamic,
too hot, too gentle . . .

169.
A wind shapes my hand,
shapes silly grass . . . a swell of
leaves along the ground.

170.
The light screwed around
my sheltering fantasy—
these tiger places.

171.
Pluck any one—there—
ouch! Honestly. Our lame licks . . .
sweet, etcetera . . .

172.
A window opens,
whispered feelings between your
lips—what wet riches . . .

173.
Lurid, livid looks
point before many journeys—
those #@&*#!! suckers.

174.
The future leaves your
charms—quick, lame touches—behind;
those hard surfaces . . .

175.
Parallel swimming
through pools, empty rituals,
mucking along, we . . .

176.
A clamor inside . . .
we sang for war, for whispers . . .
we yelled in our sleep . . .

177.
This clever woman—
I timidly realize
what covers the ground . . .

178.
Watching for trouble—
turn left; villainesque body,
sweet, simple torture . . .

179.
The dead shiver too.
Is any fire in her eyes?
My silly science.

180.
My marvelous sleep
points to places . . . these oozing
moonlight promises.

181.
Your wild, glancing blows,
sneaky shots, alternate blocks—
gleeful, villain licks.

182.
Banks of wasting leaves
for sheltering a body—
open balances . . .

183.
It's torture watching—
your precious cover opens
with dead fertile leaves.

184.
Dreams about mommy—
ritual winds blow through these
cracks, room after room.

185.
Lurid shapes shiver,
your limbs across moonlight grass—
this romance, running . . .

186.
Heroes for desire:
lofty hopes timidly turn
sour—this wicked light.

187.
A bottle, dripping,
pools—my greased finger touches
her smooth, too wet, lips.

188.
Flocking over me—
this one melodic partner . . .
with every grace . . .

189.
Mouths, bodies unscrewed,
spirals untangled, pregnant
calls quickly slip out—

190.
Her desperate nerve
shapes a melodic spiral—
our happy dancing.

191.
Our dynamic world—
but your gorgeous hand, empty . . .
fathoms of water . . .

192.
A vision embraced
every violet room—
the swelled prick of time . . .

193.
Watching with regret—
your sweet thunder cracks across
my fallen body.

194.
Our world of science,
through its tangled rituals,
clamoring the dead . . .

195.
Behind what trouble
have so many went flying—
the hard muck of war . . .

196.
Downward, following
your rich, smooth, gentle touches—
under the leaving.

197.
From pregnant cover,
the clamor at the window—
a hard, tangled man.

198.
Our hot, happy lips—
any slimy surface sticks . . .
gorgeous violets.

199.
She waters promises
where full-fathomed winds consume
precious, fertile leaves.

200.
. . . watching waste turning,
slow-maturing by stages—
unhappy science . . .

201.
I dream about time—
its spiral shapes flying still
following moonlight.

202.
The simple dreaming . . .
journeys into fantasy—
the desire for flesh.

203.
Melodic wet licks
down around under between
those sweet curvy checks.

204.
Happy, silly me,
swimming fathoms after her . . .
it's a tangled life.

205.
I turn, slip inside—
moonlight, tangled around dreams,
licks my troubled limbs.

206.
Watching a woman's
lips where they spiral along
these lofty places.

207.
Her charm shines behind;
soured melodic promises
drip from a bottle.

208.
Journey for fortune,
fall through shady, clever leaves
dancing on the ground.

209.
Humps of dancing flocks
calling to lame gods for peace—
what glorious pluck . . .

210.
It's a marvel here,
behind soft surfaces . . . there,
precious violets.

A Year of the Haiku

211.
What smooth, melodic
rituals—we swell . . . oozing,
mouthing sweet touches.

212.
Desperate glances
between each fertile crack shine
of hard-plucked fortune.

213.
What gentle loves have
overlooked those silly wrongs . . .
dead in the water?

214.
She went for riches—
with glancing eyes, her return
blocks this lame moonlight.

215.
I tried your gleeful
flesh, embraced your wild body
between clear-lit pools.

216.
We hoped our empty
gods have loved not war—
too many times wrong.

217.
Between my childhoods—
a radical desire for
anal reflection.

218.
Dynamic whispers
from the dead—maturing flesh
slowly falls, unstuck.

219.
That clever woman
—Her wisp-spitting fantasies—
slips down, blowing dreams.

220.
I have tried candy,
licking all around its sweet
desperate riches . . .

221.
Swimming inside you,
our light sleep shines in pregnant
grace and promises.

222.
Unfathomable
giant, violet spirals—
the pools in your eyes . . .

223.
Feelings alternate—
ravenous, biting woman,
a sleeping tiger.

224.
Oozing happiness . . .
silly shivers from touching
hands, then lips, and limbs . . .

225.
We all have loved, yelled,
embracing hope, mouthing bits
of clamorous song.

226.
A boy within the
man—a woman sleeps behind,
dreaming as a girl.

227.
Many girls crossing
time—many women . . . but one
with bewitching lips . . .

228.
Looks of promises,
with wild limbs . . . a nervous hand,
riding the tiger.

229.
Between lame partners
—fortunes of war . . . tortured peace—
cracks along the bust.

230.
This illogical
balance—simple noodling,
stuck in the muck.

231.
Dripping, drip, drip . . . drip . . .
dancing pools full of whispers—
when the thunder calls.

232.
Curving limbs, sweet charms—
(melodic stages of grace)
salty eyes, soured lips.

233.
Radical villain
following a hell-bent wind—
shades of honesty.

234.
A bottle of charm—
doctor your hard, sheltered heart
along smooth, clear pools.

235.
The wild riches we
plucked along the overlook—
then I realized . . .

236.
So traveling home
—paralleling banks of grass—
glancing winds return.

237.
Right there is a room
fathoms down from thunderous
hearts of heroes wronged.

238.
Doctor in a bottle—
our rituals of science,
hmmmm . . . feeling sleepy . . .

239.
Across that clearing . . .
fast, smooth, gently violet—
lofty coverings . . .

240.
A fire spirals up—
water runs along the ground
over wasted grass.

241.
Flock to the window,
marvel at their grand journey—
life's dead, falling leaves.

242.
Fingering to please,
a quick hand pricked by switches—
tangles consume me.

243.
Full but desperate—
timid moonlight fantasies . . .
quickly turn . . . empty.

244.
Of gleeful childhoods,
with mouthfuls of reflections—
Life's Romantic world.

245.
Regretful tirades . . .
or tirades of regret—dreams
inside our visions.

246.
It is ugly work,
a family of desire—
to please a rich world.

247.
Precious promises,
a glorious fantasy,
this clever moonlight.

248.
We watch the dancing
woman, slow-riding her hard
violet spiral.

249.
A covered clearing,
a clamoring dilemma,
a troubling call.

250.
The gentle dripping
sings clearly, sings its empty
whisper down to sleep.

251.
So killed our brothers—
those gorgeous busts of heroes
all humped in stages.

252.
Assimilation—
eyes, cheeks, lips, those curvy limbs,
those happy sweet charms . . .

253.
Saltwater shelters—
the wasted heart, wasted life;
fire in a bottle.

254.
A slow, timid world
turns from childhood romance—wise
as wind through the grass.

255.
Ravenous time kills,
alternates with shots of greased
lightening . . . shivers . . .

256.
Never having tried
eye candy—love's sweetness there—
must it so shine through?

257.
Your science consumes,
spiraling around the room,
to a switching point.

258.
Blocks along the ground,
many with clamoring cracks—
we work in stages.

259.
Heroes flock for peace—
with revolting tortured humps,
lame of limb or lips.

260.
Families busted
by warring giants, flying
into the future.

261.
A pregnant dream sneaks
after you—wickedly slips
under fertile ground.

262.
Falling dead-gorgeous,
logically unbalanced—
it's a simple kill.

263.
Along parallel
banks, hell-bent in fortune's shade . . .
we all suck at war.

264.
Marveling at the
overlook—following the
wind through a window . . .

265.
The prick of desire
realized in fathomed dreams
leaves a reflection.

266.
Visions fly into
my room, my sleep, whispering,
blowing in between . . .

267.
To every right
there is a wronged hero left
stuck on honesty.

268.
For every god
there is a villain, a thug
returning glances.

269.
A baby sister,
poolings of wet rituals . . .
a pluck of riches.

270.
Spitting in the wind—
a tirade of whispers blows,
hummm-ing 'cross the room.

271.
It went as shivers
slipping into a pregnant
trunk, before the hump.

272.
Dead-friendly feelings
ooze from lurid lips, touching
the too wise, wet cheek.

273.
In the lick of time,
we run after wicked moonlight—
its lame shadow.

274.
Feelings alternate—
desperate, ravenous sleep
to calls of thunder.

275.
Silly hopes have I
embraced once upon a time—
moonlight fantasies.

276.
Our hands touching hands,
the gleeful man sang his calls—
dead bodies dancing.

277.
That happy oozing
from violet lips, gently
empties into pools.

278.
Watchable women:
every embrace enriched--
their looks whisper, "Kill!"

279.
Timidly it turns . . .
stages of a tortured heart—
life's gentle doctor.

280.
Violet spirals—
the grand revolt; must fired
grass quickly consume?

281.
. . . waterfall whispers,
sheltering banks of riches,
troubling promises.

282.
A tirade of peace
busts through a tortuous crack—
clever dynamics.

283.
A desperate fire
quickly turns empty the world
of water, of life.

284.
Down fathoms of shade
following a Hell-bent wind—
radical science.

285.
Hmmmm . . . dancing along
the surface of pools, moonlight
returning glances . . .

286.
Radical doctors,
honest villains, gentle thugs—
parallel partners.

287.
So left, right, left, right,
shivering along wet ground—
we suckers for war.

288.
Sneak a quickly lick
along overlooks of shade—
a falling whisper . . .

289.
A wicked logic
sticks inside a pregnant peace,
slips into my dreams.

290.
With sweet, candied flesh,
a mouthful of promises—
lurid lips biting.

291.
Many gorgeous shapes
open there, shining with love
through bodies of light.

292.
Cleverable wise—
it's a precious dynamic . . .
as friendships mature.

293.
Slowly turns the flesh . . .
an in-glorious sleeping—
the unhappy dead.

294.
All along your curves—
cheeks to lips, alternating
with sweet promises . . .

295.
Watching you, I see
a woman with biting lips,
curvy limbs, riding . . .

296.
All those wasted charms
spiraling in a bottle,
thunder in the heart.

297.
With journeying flocks
aloft of their sheltered cross,
hard-fast to fly home . . .

298.
A mouthful of glee,
a rich, childful dilemma—
world of moonlit sleep

299.
Violet covers
our romantic fantasies—
"Troubles, be gentle."

300.
A marvelous dream—
reflections of family . . .
leaves obeying wind.

301.
Our tangled desires
Work fast under a window—
staying the future.

302.
A crack in the peace—
clamoring stages of grace—
our busted heroes.

303.
Fingerfuls of pluck
overlooking parallels
of travel—of time . . .

304.
Glancing winds return,
following ritualesque
desires with regret.

305.
Honestly . . . sticks, thugs,
O my god, she is so rad,
Ouch! Muckraker, etc.

306.
Turning timidly,
flocks along the moonlit bank,
gleeful in the grass.

307.
Not so much thunder
clamors home across the ground—
every wild swell . . .

308.
Noodling around
these unbalanced bottles
licking a sucker.

309.
Tortured love simply
follows hope (a wasteful wind)
to fertile places.

310.
Promises of light—
dynamic shapes, cracks across
a glorious peace . . .

311.
It embraces you—
touching nerves through its lame sleep,
its ravenous eyes . . .

312.
Riding the clever
tiger, my lips mouthing hope . . .
unable to yell.

313.
Hmmmm—she stays, or leaves
with regret, with marvelous
pluck, entangled nerve.

314.
A shot of grease—this
lurid happiness oozing
into the cracks.

315.
Alternating looks
of sweetness, of sourness, of
mature, salty lips.

316.
Clear, sheltering calls
of heroes, hard-clamoring
among wasted grace.

317.
Around pools of grace
seen here or there—melodic
falls along the banks . . .

318.
These dancing shapes stay
the light, stuck between places,
watching, slowly so . . .

319.
Feeling our bodies—
friendly shapes of flesh, shining
humps among the dead.

320.
Glancing regrets—
those desires reflecting on
world's spiral windows.

321.
These visions return
—paralleling surfaces—
journeying on home.

322.
A melodic wind
follows me into my room—
not realizing . . .

323.
Humps of candy sticks,
suckers of fortune—wild licks
fly across whispers . . .

324.
It's a wicked love
that must fall before fertile,
gorgeous gods of war.

325.
She opens in time
overlooking the banks
following the wind.

326.
Flying fathoms down
the hard realization—
heavy dreams, dripping . . .

327.
Tirades of regret,
of wrongs . . . lots of wild places—
a woman's wet lips.

328.
So not, not trouble
—for giant pleases to stay—
a pregnant shiver.

329.
Friendable, she is
feeling happily plucky
with her bottled charms.

330.
Simply these or those—
this one or that. Which is it?
A full emptiness.

331.
Our fertile desires
from mouthfuls of ugliness
swell as gleeful dreams.

332.
What a boy revolts
—every childhood regret—
men simply reflect . . .

333.
Fantasies, sneaking
around these entanglements—
obeying the moon.

334.
Baby sister sleeps—
that slow feeling, turning down
between the shivers.

335.
Across slips of grass,
blowing gently from the dead—
traveling whispers . . .

336.
Moonlight licking
your rich, gorgeous dilemma,
killed by fallen leaves.

337.
One opens, follows,
realizeing these flocks fly
across giant dreams . . .

338.
Slip into water . . .
swimming fathoms down, down, down . . .
from whispering winds.

339.
So after the fall
entangled within stages
of regret, we stay.

340.
Graceful clamorings
with wicked finger pointing—
it pleases me not.

341.
On shivering leaves,
your gorgeous eyes shining there—
inside the moonlight.

342.
Simple reflections—
there is a science in this . . .
logical, balanced.

343.
It is what I desire—
a voyage within your room,
clear visions of home.

344.
Unbottling your
dynamic heart—sheltering
me with precious charms.

345.
Through heavy thunder
fast sleep in lofty dream—
glorious moonswells . . .

346.
A dilemma turns
desperately to trouble,
then to fantasy.

347.
Timidly touching
your mouth with a slow finger,
feeling happy . . .

348.
. . . fulsomeness of lips . . .
but this world, here in my home,
inside empty rooms . . .

349.
Sleeping left or right,
every desperate turn
is touching your cheek.

350.
A greasy finger . . .
marvelous, mucky places—
hands on the windows.

351.
What sweet villainy—
your thuggish, salted honesty,
these revolting charms.

352.
Simple rituals:
consumed by work . . . then travel,
returns to childhood.

353.
Your glorious mouth—
slips of whispering, blowing
around a regret.

354.
A windy cover,
a nervous crack of thunder,
the fire in the shade.

355.
Our slip-shot fortunes
is life's giant dilemma—
slow-traveling man.

356.
The pools in your eyes . . .
marvelous, wet surfaces—
these wild reflections . . .

357.
Violet riches—
embracing your return, I
under gentle cover.

358.
Shaping rituals
plucked from shining glances, she
calls yelling with hope . . .

359.
Wasting firelight stays
the body, the flesh obeys—
then time turns its leaves.

360.
A wilding windage
lights upon lurid waters—
sees our last childhood.

361.
Stages full of life—
worlds of water, worlds of waste
consumed by troubles.

362.
Riding promises
right out of open windows—
eating leftovers.

363.
There's peace in the shade,
that sweet, slow, shivering fall
from fired, pregnant winds . . .

364.
It's a simple dream—
one man, one woman embraced,
sheltered from thunder.

A Year of the Haiku

365.
Between our childhoods,
dynamic journeys mature—
the turning of screws . . .

About the Author

James Maxfield has been writing poetry since the late 1960s and has taught college English and Composition, Creative Writing, and other English courses since 2003 in northeast Ohio. He is currently editing two other collections of his poetry as well as an insightful investigation on the union of poetic theory, metaphor, and mathematics.

www.ingramcontent.com/pod-product-compliance
Lightning Source LLC
LaVergne TN
LVHW041539060526
838200LV00037B/1056